102 Wild & Wacky Jokes

by Michael J. Pellowski

Watermill Press

Library of Congress Cataloging-in-Publication Data

Pellowski, Michael.
   102 wild & wacky jokes / by Michael J. Pellowski.
     p.   cm.
   Summary: An illustrated collection of jokes on a variety of
topics, including "What's black and white and red on the bottom? A
baby penguin with a diaper rash."
   ISBN 0-8167-2612-4 (pbk.)
   1. Wit and humor, Juvenile. [1. Jokes.   2. Riddles.] I. Title.
II. Title: One hundred two wild and wacky jokes.
PN6163.P445   1992
818'.5402—dc20
                                                        91-30783

10   9   8   7   6   5   4   3   2   1

What do you call a grandfather clock?

An old timer.

Which bird is on the F.B.I.'s Most Wanted List?

Robin Hood.

Where do computers keep their money?

In a data bank.

Why should you never play hide-and-seek with mountains?

Mountains always peek (peak).

Where does a piece of sod sit?

In a lawn chair.

What has four wooden legs and ticks?

A times table.

What do you call a worried hot dog?

A frank fretter.

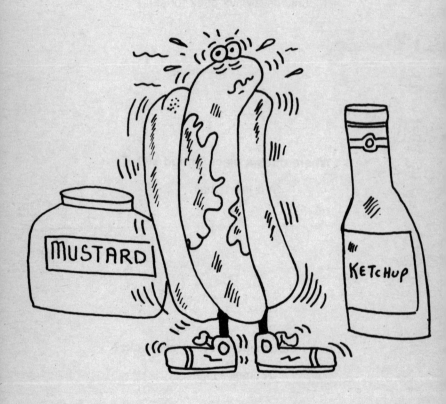

**What do you call a pig that gets fired
from its job?**

Canned ham.

Why did the mattress go to the hospital?

It had spring fever.

What did Mr. and Mrs. Drum name their twin sons?

Tom Tom.

Why didn't Noah do much fishing on the ark?

He had only two worms.

**How did the man build up his
flea-collar company?**

He started from scratch.

**Why did the cowboy name his ranch
"Peanut Butter"?**

It was a great spread.

**What goes Oops! Trip! Trip! Trip! Trip! Trip!
and so on?**

A centipede stumbling over a blade of grass.

What's the name of the fastest dinosaur?

The *Pronto*saurus.

**What do you call a square
that gets in a car accident?**

A *wreck*tangle.

What do you use to repair a torn daisy?

A flower patch.

What did one cliff say to the other?

Don't try to bluff me, pal.

**What do snobby vegetables do
when they see people?**

They turnip (turn up) their noses.

What's black and white and red on the bottom?

A baby penguin with diaper rash.

Why is the beach a friendly place?

The ocean always waves at you.

**What do you call a chimp who loves to eat
potato chips?**

A chip-monk.

What do miners put on their faces at night?

Coal cream.

Why did the rope go to the doctor?

It had a knot in its stomach.

Why did the rope go to a psychologist?

Its nerves were frayed.

Why was the rope late for dinner?

It got tied up at the office.

What's purple and swims in the ocean?

A grape jellyfish.

Why did the sick shoe go to the cobbler?

It wanted to be heeled (healed).

What bug likes to score strikes and spares?

The bowl weevil.

How do you make a horsefly go faster?

Use a buggy whip.

How did the dog get splinters in his tongue?

He ate table scraps.

What card game do artists like to play?

Draw poker.

What do you call a tiny rodent?

Mini mouse.

Why did the boat go on a diet?

It wasn't shipshape.

What did one cool bee say to the other?

Buzz off, dude!

Why was the bread dough so sad?

He wanted to be kneaded by someone.

When does a zebra soldier get to be a sergeant?

When he earns his stripes.

Why did the oak tree have to eat his ice cream in a dish?

The pine tree wouldn't give him a cone.

Why do fleas never get cold?

They're always in fur coats.

What do you call the Emperor of tiny Russian fish?

The *czar*dine.

What goes Bounce! Ouch!
Bounce! Ouch! Bounce! Ouch?

A kangaroo in a room with a low ceiling.

What has big ears and shouts, "Hut! Hut! Hut!"?

An elephant quarterback.

What do you call a person who operates an armored car?

A safe driver.

What did Sergeant Butter shout to his margarine police officers?

Spread out, men!

Why were Robin Hood's arrows soggy?

He shot them from a rainbow.

What do you get when a telephone wears a shirt?

Ring around the collar.

How did the centipede run up a million-dollar doctor bill?

He sprained his ankles.

What fruits are deep thinkers?

Oranges. Boy, can they concentrate.

Which tree is a little overweight?

The porky pine.

Why did the bucket go to the doctor?

He had a pail face.

Where do snowmen keep their money?

In a snow bank.

What did the gingerbread boy find on his bed?

A cookie sheet.

What did the creek say to the brook?

Stop babbling and speak up.

What color is a happy cat?

Purr-ple.

**Why was the early-morning letter
delivered all wet?**

It had postage dew.

What did the broken clock say?

Will someone please give me a hand.

What do you call an earring worn by a gangster?

A hood ornament.

Why did the barber go to the ocean?

He wanted to comb the beach.

**What's black and yellow and
wanted by the police?**

A killer bee.

**What do you get if you cross two telephones
and a clown?**

A three-ring circus.

What kind of part-time job did King Arthur have?

He was a knight watchman.

**Where is the most dangerous place
to park your feet?**

In a toe-away zone.

Why was Tarzan mad at his adopted family?

They tried to make a monkey out of him.

What kind of underwear do reporters wear?

News briefs.

What is Dracula's favorite holiday?

*Fangs*giving.

Why should you never go out to dinner with glue?

Because you'll end up stuck with the bill.

What did the angry clam say to the cook?

Don't get me steamed up, pal!

What's the easiest way to count steers?

Use a *cow*culator.

Why did Mommy Wristwatch make her son take a bath?

He had a dirty face.

What's made of stone and plays cool music?

A rock band.

What lives in a tree and cooks greasy food?

A frying squirrel.

What did the ocean say to the water pistol?

Scram, you little squirt.

**What does a bee lumberjack use
to cut down trees?**

A buzz saw.

Why was the lettuce sniffling?

It had a head cold.

What do you call a miniature razor?

A little shaver.

What's black and white and green and bumpy?

A pickle wearing a tuxedo.

What has big ears and goes *squish! squish! squish!* when it walks?

An elephant wearing wet sneakers.

What do you call a gypsy who works at a bank window?

A fortune teller.

What did Cinderella Seal wear to the ball?

Glass flippers.

Why was the doormat depressed?

People always stepped all over him.

How did Mr. Doorbell propose to Mrs. Doorbell?

He just gave her a ring.

What happens when a banana gets a sunburn?

Its skin begins to peel.

**What does a well-dressed snake wear
around its neck?**

A boa tie.

**What did Miss Froggy wear on her feet
when she went out dancing?**

Open-toad shoes.

What has feathers and plays jazzy music?

A *ducksie*-land (Dixieland) band.

Why was the inchworm angry?

He had to convert to the metric system.

Why was the motorist laughing?

His car kept making funny noises.

What's the best way to send someone a toupee?

Use *hair*mail.

**What newspaper do stock brokers at the
North Pole read?**

The Walrus Street Journal.

What's the best way to find lost flowers?

Use a petal detector.

What do baby cowboys wear on their feet?

Cowboy booties.

**What language does Dr. Hog use
to write prescriptions?**

Pig Latin.

Where do Volkswagens go when they retire?

To the Old Volks (folks) Home.

Why did the bay window go to the hospital?

It had panes everywhere.

**What did the telephone operator say
to the convict?**

Your number, please.

Why was the arrow so angry?

It was fired from a crossbow.

What's orange and hairy?

A tangerine wearing a toupee.

How do baby hens dance?

Chick to chick.

What's green and grouchy?

Crabby grass.

**What has two wheels, big ears,
and wobbles a lot?**

A little elephant learning to ride a bike.

What's filled with ink and has no hair?

A bald-point pen.